Specially commissioned by

FILTER CIGARETTES

Published by Queen Anne Press,
Paulton House, Shepherdess Walk,
London, N.1.

Printed and bound in Great Britain
by Hazell Watson & Viney Ltd,
Aylesbury, Bucks

HISTORY OF
HALL-MARKS

by
Wynyard R. T. Wilkinson

ACKNOWLEDGMENTS

My grateful thanks to the following for allowing use of their material and providing information:

Mr J. S. Forbes and Miss Hare of the Worshipful Company of Goldsmiths

Mrs M. MacAleer, The Antiques Supermarket, Barrett Street, London, W.1

Jeremy Syms

Cedric A. Nixon (Photographer) 9 Huguenot Place, London, S.W.18

Messrs Wigham, Richardson & Bevington, Insurance Brokers

CONTENTS

Editor's Note

Written primarily for those interested in collecting British silver, this book touches only briefly on how to recognise the period and place of origin of that most regal metal, gold. This is deliberate in that first, antique gold is far beyond the reach of most of our pockets and second, it is an increasingly rare commodity.

Although a system of hall-marking gold developed upon similar lines to that of silver, very little of the precious metal was ever mined in England, whilst the majority of British silver was literally 'home grown'. Consequently most of the gold used in this country was imported so it became impossible to regulate the standard. This led to the actual physical stamping of the caratage upon the gold piece: 9, 12, 15, 18 or 22 carat—though the latter is no longer used in this country.

For those who still wish to 'place' great great grandfather's gold watch it is of value to consult the silver tables as the town mark on gold is usually, though not always, the same as on silver. For a more accurate attribution we would recommend approaching a reputable dealer.

THE GOLDSMITHS

THE GOLDSMITHS

In order to reap the full rewards from an interest such as silver collecting it is a good idea to know something of the background to the origin and manufacture of the item to be examined. Surprisingly enough silver mining in Europe can be traced back to 4000 B.C. It seems that at first lead only was mined, as silver was not then in demand as a precious metal. However during the next thousand years silver, probably because of its lustre, came into use for coinage. Both silver and gold have been mined in Britain since Roman times and, although even then they were not to be found in sufficient quantities to make their extraction really profitable, mining of these metals continued up to the early eighteenth century, when silver mined in both Wales and Lancaster was in use for coinage.

The extraction and purification of silver from the many and varying ores in which it is found is both technically complicated and of little relevance to our purpose. However, it is useful to have some idea of the work involved in producing an ingot of silver from the rough ore.

The silversmith of antiquity simply burnt his lump of galena until he was left with lead oxide and a small piece of silver. A subsequent development was to heat the galena slowly until the lead melted at its lower melting point, leaving a lump of silver. More modern processes were developed during the last century. One is really a method of production by electrolysis, from which large quantities of 100 per cent pure silver may be obtained. Another process allows the silver to amalgamate with another metal, zinc, thus separating it from the lead in which it is embedded. The new alloy is then distilled producing almost pure silver.

After the ingot silver has been obtained the next important factor influencing the finished product is the maker. Apart from causing the occasional 'Oh really, how interesting' at parties the silversmith of today is not regarded as much more than a refined

4

form of artist. This has not always been the case, however. Indeed during the centuries of Viking supremacy in England the silversmith was a leading citizen of the highest order. And after the Norman conquest he took on a new role in society. His much-needed business acumen—which often led him to not only make silver and jewellery, but to act as banker and pawnbroker as well —made him very valuable to a form of government which was seriously lacking in economic understanding. His technical and administrative powers, together with his artistic prowess meant that at a time when government was becoming increasingly complicated he was one of the few citizens able to comprehend its intricacies. These achievements gave the silversmith a position of power, and he was to be found as much administering new building projects and the workers at the mint, as he was producing plate for the houses of the nobility.

This power gave rise to the formation by 1180 of a silversmiths' guild in London, which was almost immediately fined by the King's Court for being established without the King's licence. The Guild was, however, powerful enough by this time to ignore the order to pay the fine, and it appears that it was in fact never paid. In 1238, in retaliation for substandard plate being sold to the Royal Household, Henry III commanded that six 'discreet' silversmiths, known as wardens, be appointed to ensure the correct behaviour of the other member silversmiths: there are still wardens at Goldsmiths' Hall* to this day.

In a power struggle as early as 1267 the members of the Goldsmiths' Company had a pitched battle with the members of the Taylors' Company. Some 500 men were involved in the fight many of whom were neither Goldsmiths nor Taylors but paid rabble. The result of this affray is uncertain but it is known that the bodies of the dead on both sides were thrown into the Thames, and that those unfortunates arrested by the militia were hanged as a warning to others.

*The word goldsmith incorporates both gold- and silversmiths—a goldsmith is by necessity a silversmith, and likewise a silversmith is qualified to work in gold. From here onward the term goldsmith may be understood to mean a working member of a goldsmith guild.

During the following two and a half centuries the goldsmiths continued to flourish: before 1524 there were no less than 17 goldsmith Lord Mayors of London. The demand for their wares was gradually changing from the ecclesiastical to the secular as more traders accumulated private wealth.

The next important incident in the history of the Guild occurred about 1540, when the demands of the Reformation forced the Goldsmiths to destroy the effigy of their patron saint, St. Dunstan, which decorated the entrance to Goldsmiths' Hall. The full consequences of the Reformation on the Guild are difficult to measure, but the dissolution of the monasteries did provide a surplus of church plate, and despite their desire for visible signs of the changed order, the new church leaders were very practical when it came to ordering expensive new plate. They merely sent off the old chalices and had them converted to communion cups, thus saving a great deal of expense.

However, thanks to the extravagant fashion set by Henry VIII, the Royal Court was engaged in a form of competition as to who had the best plate after the King, which was followed immediately by the diplomatic necessity of giving massive pieces of plate to foreign governments (an example of this is the huge quantity of Elizabethan plate in Russia). In all a great deal of important plate was fashioned in the sixteenth century.

The first 50 years of the seventeenth century were bordering on disaster for the Goldsmiths' Company: they had to sell plate to pay a forced loan to the Royal Exchequer and their Guildhall was used by Parliament as its exchequer during the Civil War. The war was equally disastrous for the individual smiths: when both sides were crying out for plate to melt down to pay their troops there was little or no demand for new plate. The end of the war only worsened the goldsmiths' predicament as the new puritanical leadership forbade the manufacture of decorative ware. In complete contrast to pre-war taste, the goldsmith had to keep his wares absolutely plain, or face huge fines or imprisonment.

Happily for the goldsmith, fortunes changed with the Restoration and he found himself the supplier of a much wanted commodity. The great families had sacrificed vast amounts of silver to the cause of war, and now in a period of rising prosperity and apparent peace needed to replace the table grandeur which they had so long been without. An additional factor was the middle class who had now reached a stage when status was defined by exterior wealth, and silver, even if very much lighter than that used by the nobility, was a very good way of impressing new found affluence upon a neighbour. This market, combined with the traditional ones of Church and State, led to a dramatic expansion in the craft which continued unhindered through to the nineteenth century.

The last, and probably most important influence on both the smiths and their work was the immigration in the late seventeenth and early eighteenth centuries of a large number of religious refugees, the Huguenots. These men were generally very fine craftsmen, using designs and techniques far in advance of the protected English smiths. They brought continental thought and line to the English arts which were quickly adopted by their patrons, causing their English rivals to update their own attitude or go out of business.

The eighteenth century, and the beginning of the Industrial Revolution saw the role of the goldsmith ceasing to be that of an important member of society, and becoming increasingly that of just another member of the new order of worker-craftsmen. This changing role, however, did not prevent goldsmiths of superb brilliance emerging, either as specialist smiths producing large quantities of a top quality product as well as the normal wares, or as master craftsmen whose work is, even to the uninitiated, of far superior design and execution to that of their contemporaries. These men and women may be regarded as the last of the real goldsmiths, as they, like so many other craftsmen were to be absorbed into the world of machine and workshop.

HALL-MARKS

Although marks are found on Roman and
Byzantine silver indicating that some form
of quality control system was then in use, it
was not until 1238 that any form of legal
control was introduced in England. This
Ordinance not only provided for six wardens
to superintend the goldsmiths' work in London, but also set out the acceptable stan-
dards of fineness for both gold and silver.

The next important Act was that of 1300
which purported to influence 'All goldsmiths of England, and anywhere else in the
King's dominion'. It laid down that the
standard for gold should be 19½ carats and
the silver standard the same as for coin; this
was 'Sterling', a fineness of 925 parts silver
per 1000 parts, or 11 oz 2 pennyweights
Troy pure silver to every 12 oz Troy. The
Act further mentioned that no vessel of
silver 'was to depart from the hands of the
workers' until it had been assayed by one of

the guardians and marked with a leopard's head. This was the first of the marks and the direct ancestor of the marks in use today.

The 1300 Act also ruled that 'in all the good towns in England where there are goldsmiths, they shall make the same statutes as those of London (are) making and that one (man) shall go from each town for all the others to London to seek (or to fetch) their sure touch ... if any goldsmith shall do otherwise than aforesaid it is ordained he be punished by prison and by ransom at the King's will'. It was not made clear whether the intention was that the leopard's head should be used in the provinces as well as London or not, neither did it clarify whether the supervision was entirely the responsibility of the London Goldsmiths' Guild. It was not until 1856 that this Ordinance was repealed, having been in force for well over 550 years.

Ordinances and Statutes relating to gold and silver are almost unique in that even after being repealed they cannot be considered as irrelevant as the wares produced under them will certainly have survived the Acts themselves and must be considered lawful so long as they conform to the regulations in force at the time of their manufacture.

In 1327 the Goldsmiths' Guild received its first Royal Charter, in which it was given the power to enforce the laws of the realm with which it was concerned with the aid of the Mayor and Sheriffs of the City of London. The next 100 years saw a number of further statutes relating to the goldsmiths, including the provision for each smith to have a mark to be placed on a finished item *after* the piece had been assayed. These statutes also have all been repealed.

The next important development was the Statute of 1423, where it is set out that no 'workmanship of silver' is to be 'set to sale' in the City of London without previously being marked with a leopard's head and the sign or mark of the worker who made it. So, within 200 years of the first statute, the City of London had developed a system which included the assay, a hall-mark (the mark of the Guild's Hall), and a maker's mark.

In 1462 the Goldsmiths' Guild was

invested with power, as a corporate body, to use a seal and hold land in its own right, and to search, inspect, try and regulate all gold and silver offered for sale throughout England. In addition to these powers, in 1504 the Goldsmiths' Company was allowed to imprison and fine defaulters and to seize unlawful pieces; it is still the practice for the Assay Office to seize sub-standard or 'fake' wares and ensure that they are not offered for sale.

In 1478 an additional mark—a plain letter to be changed at the end of each Goldsmiths' year—was added to the leopard's head and maker's mark. The purpose of the 'variable date letter' was to make it possible to distinguish not only who made a piece, but also in which year. This was to discourage corruption at the Assay Office as a dated piece could always be traced to a particular Assay Master.

When Henry VIII debased the coinage in 1544 the Goldsmiths' Company deemed it necessary to reassure its patrons that the standard of wrought plate itself had not also been debased, and in order to make a clear differentiation a new mark was introduced, a 'lion passant guardant'. This mark was probably one of the most successful commercial guarantees ever devised, as there are today many people who, with good reason, will not believe a piece is silver unless it bears the lion passant mark.

Thus the hall-mark series that is found on silver assayed at London today developed.

Legislation brought in around 1575 begins with a long recital concerning the 'abuses in gold smythes ... to the great defraudings of her Majestie and her good subjects'. This is probably the most remarkable of all the statutes in that it demands the minimum standard for wrought gold to be increased to 22 carats, the highest practical, while silver is kept at sterling standard. The statute ruled that a maker's mark be put onto silver before being sold or exchanged but did not mention hall-marks directly. An interesting reflection on this statute and its effects is that, when in 1643 the Royalists decided upon a policy of forced loans to subsidise their treasury, an alternative was offered of providing silver plate in lieu, the rate for which was 5s an ounce for marked plate, and 4s 4d an ounce for plate bearing only the maker's mark. This seems to indicate that it was not unusual to have unmarked silver and that it was certainly not considered illegal to sell plate bearing only the maker's mark.

The next statute was the result of the culmination of the huge demand for silver at the latter end of the seventeenth century and the long overdue new coinage. These two factors led to a wholesale melting of the old coin to convert it to plate, which in turn caused a shortage of sterling standard silver for the new coinage. The statute simply raised the required standard to 958·3 parts pure silver per 1000 parts, or 11 oz 10 pennyweights to every 12 Troy ounces. This new standard was called the *Britannia Standard*, and it was made compulsory for two new hall-marks to be used, the lion's head erased and the figure of Britannia*, in addition to the date letter. At the same time it was declared that the maker's mark should be the first two letters of the maker's surname.

*

It was not until 1720 that the old Sterling Standard was reinstated, although provision was made for the voluntary continuation of the Britannia Standard—it is still possible to buy modern Britannia Standard silver in London today. With the return of the old standard, a tax of 6d an ounce was introduced, and this led to a number of dishonest practices on the part of goldsmiths engaged on large pieces of plate. As the tax was collected when a piece of plate was assayed there were two main methods of circumventing the tax: one was to take the mark off a piece of plate due to be scrapped and weld this into the new piece, the other was to send a small piece to be assayed, and then use the small piece in the construction of the larger. The 1720 Statute also provided for the maker's mark to revert to being the first letters of the maker's christian and surnames.

The duty was removed for a period in 1758, but when it was reintroduced in 1784 a mark representing the king's head was added to the other marks to indicate that the duty had been paid. For the first 18 months the mark was intaglio, incuse as opposed to the other marks which are in cameo.

One of the scarcest and most interesting marks, the 'drawback' mark, was introduced in 1784. This was a form of export rebate. If a piece of plate on which the duty had been paid was exported the goldsmith was able to reclaim the duty, and from December 1784 to July 1785 a mark of a standing figure of Britannia* was used to show that this was the case. However, as most often the piece had been fully marked and finished before the application of the drawback mark, it was not unusual for the mark to cause expensive or unsightly damage which had to be rectified before the piece was sent to its new owner.

There have been very many statutes concerning silver since 1800, but these have tended to lean toward the technical rather than the practical rendering them of little interest to the collector.

*

THE PROVINCES

The Statute of 1423 provided for the granting of 'divers touches' to seven English towns: Bristol, Coventry, Lincoln, Newcastle upon Tyne, Norwich, Salisbury and York. Chester is omitted from the list, probably because it was under the direct supervision of the Earl of Chester, and Parliament considered this to be good enough. To find some definite connection between these towns is difficult, but a major factor in their choice was probably that they were all centres of communication, thus making it easy for plate to be brought to them from the towns around for assay.

These towns continued to operate alongside a number of smaller towns whose guilds and smiths had developed their own system of marking until the introduction of the Britannia Standard in 1696, when provincial assaying seems to suddenly come to a halt.* To remedy this lack of provincial involvement, the Plate Assay Act of 1700 was passed which set up Assay Offices in towns where the mints had been started in 1696: Bristol, Chester, Exeter, Norwich and York. This Act omitted Newcastle upon Tyne but, after representations from the smiths of that town the omission was rectified in 1702.

Of these five towns neither Bristol nor Norwich appear to have had enough smiths to sustain an Assay Office, while the other towns took a civic symbol as their identifying mark or Town mark. Probably for the same reason as Bristol and Norwich the York Office was closed in 1717, leaving just Chester, Exeter and Newcastle outside London. In 1721, with the return to the old standard, these three offices all reintroduced a leopard's head, as well as the lion passant to replace the Britannia symbol, alongside the town and makers' marks.

One of the fiercest political battles ever

---

* Perhaps because the local smiths were recruited to work in the mints that were established to produce the 'new coinage', and to facilitate a quick and efficient change-over by both increasing the production and spreading the distribution through the country.

fought by the Goldsmiths' Company happened in 1772. This concerned the proposition, supported by many important and influential goldsmiths and civic leaders, to open two new Assay Offices at Birmingham and Sheffield. New methods of manufacturing silver by machine processes had been developed by both Birmingham and Sheffield who were faced with the dangerous problem of sending wares on long journeys to assay towns to be tested, marked and then returned without any guarantee that the marked goods would be sufficiently well wrapped to make the return journey unharmed.

Two committees were set up by Parliament to examine the proposition. They were petitioned by the London Goldsmiths' Company to reject the proposals on the grounds that the general standard of silver would be threatened, and that as neither of the towns had a Goldsmiths' Guild, there would be no official body to protect the trade from malpractices. However the controversial Assay Offices were opened in 1773, taking their marks not from their town arms as had been traditional, but from the public house in the Strand where much of the lobbying for the bill had been conducted, The Crown and Anchor: Sheffield adopted the Crown and Birmingham the Anchor. A few years later the office at York was reopened.

The following 80 years saw little change in the form of the provincial offices, and due to stricter enforcement of the hall-marking laws and the improvement in communication, it became exceptional for a goldsmith not to send his wares to the nearest Assay Office regardless of the magnitude or insignificance of the piece.

With the shifting of population from the rural districts to the new industrial towns in the first quarter of the nineteenth century, the smaller Assay Offices found the demand for their services dwindling as the local goldsmiths either retired and were not replaced, or left for the glamour and increased prosperity of town life. As a result of this exodus the revenue at both Exeter and Newcastle from charges for assay was, by 1880, not enough to cover the cost of keeping the office open and in 1882 Exeter was shut, followed two years later by Newcastle. In some instances, however, such as York, this was not so much the case, as the Assay Office there only really received work from one workshop from its reopening in 1776 until it was closed as the result of an enquiry in 1856.

Chester continued to mark silver until 1962 when, in agreement with the recommendations of the Departmental Committee on Hall-marking, the office was closed. It is interesting that in the years preceding the closure, over 90 per cent of the plate assayed at Chester was of Birmingham manufacture.

The remaining offices—Birmingham, London and Sheffield—are all kept busy enough today to justify their remaining open and, if anything, the modern trend is towards more new silver rather than less. For the Silver Jubilee of King George V in 1935 various manufacturers sold sets of teaspoons, each one marked at a different Assay Office.

SCOTLAND

The history of the Scottish goldsmiths, their craft, and their Assay Offices is very different from that of the English smiths, primarily because of the scattered distribution of the relatively small population. The Scottish goldsmiths developed quite independently of their English neighbours, almost it seems in deliberate contrast, for while the style of the English wares was quite distinct from those of the continent, the Scottish ware was often almost indistinguishable from the equivalent pieces made simultaneously in Holland and France.

As early as 1457, a statute was enacted 'to eschew the deceiving done to the Kings Lieges', appointing 'a cunning man of gude conscience quhick sall be Deakone of the the craft' who, as an additional safeguard was to place his mark alongside that of the maker if it were of the required quality. This quality was different for both gold and silver from that required of the English smiths; the standard for gold being 20 carats, that for silver 'xi grains fine', which is 11 oz pure silver to every 12 oz Troy or 916·6 parts per 1000.

Unlike England, provision was made for towns with only one goldsmith that he should take his work to the 'head officiates of the towne', who were responsible for placing a mark indicating the name of the town near the maker's mark. This legislation, although apparently foolproof was still open to abuse, so in order to cut down on the malpractices a follow-up statute was introduced 16 years later. This attempted to undo the harm done by some goldsmiths 'myning too much laye with their silver'. It was made compulsory for each town with a goldsmith, or smiths, to appoint a Warden and a Deacon to test all the silver produced in that town. They had to put their marks jointly on every piece found up to standard (our phrase 'up to scratch' is derived from the scratching of silver in order to make an assay), while confiscating every piece which was found to be substandard.

The law then remained static, apart from minor amendments, through to 1555 when the gold standard was raised to 22 carats, and the silver standard 'restored' to 916·6. This implies that the accepted standard had fallen below this level. In 1586 the Deacon and Master of the Goldsmiths' Craft (Guild) were granted their first Letters Patent which, in effect, gave them the same power in Scotland as was enjoyed by the London Goldsmiths' Company. In contrast to the London Goldsmiths' Company, the Edinburgh goldsmiths had previously belonged to the Hammermen, the guild for all metal workers, regardless of whether they were blacksmiths, pewterers or goldsmiths.

The Edinburgh goldsmiths adopted the castle as their mark, and appear to have been very strict in their supervision, as in the years immediately after their charter they fined or confiscated plate from a great number of the local smiths. From 1681, there is a date letter added to the other three marks of town, maker and Deacon.

With the Act of Union in 1707, provision was made for the laws relating to hall-marking 'to remain in the same force as before ... but they to be alterable by the parliament of Great Britain'. This ruling was to cause the Scottish goldsmiths some discomforture. In 1719 when the Britannia Standard became optional and a duty of sixpence an ounce was introduced, the English goldsmiths were fortunate in that they were offered the concession of using less fine and thus less expensive, plate, in exchange for the burden of the new tax. In Scotland however, where the Britannia Standard had never been used, the effect of the first measure was nil and that of the second bordering on the disastrous: in order to compensate for the new duty the smiths had to raise the price of their plate, the result of which was a significant drop in demand.

The subsequent Acts applied equally to Scotland as to England until 1819 when, in a statute, 27 Goldsmiths were named and incorporated into the 'Glasgow Goldsmiths' Company'. They were to elect four Wardens annually and were allotted the mark of a lion rampant to go alongside the town mark, duty paid mark, variable date letter and maker's mark. What was extraordinary was that the statute laid down that the acceptable standard should be 'Sterling' (925), which was the first time that the standard required in Scotland had been raised above 916·6. Thus on one side of the country was Edinburgh, which had been autonomous until this statute, and required a standard of 916·6, while on the other side was the newly appointed office in Glasgow which required 925 standard. This was responsible for the smuggling, even by some of the largest Glasgow goldsmiths, of the lower standard plate to Edinburgh, and subsequently underusage of the Glasgow Assay Office. It was not until 1836 that this situation was rectified when it was made obligatory for the minimum standard for the United Kingdom to be 925. This evened the balance, and from 1836 onward a very great amount of plate was assayed in Glasgow.

Scotland, due to the small size and remoteness of many of the townships, and the great risk of transporting plate for assay, is unique in that almost every 'burgh' had a smith, and it was the rule rather than the exception for him to make his own marks. The most important of these 'burghs' are Aberdeen, Banff, Dundee, Greenock, Inverness and Perth. A study of these towns and the history of their craftsmen is both absorbing and complex, but as their wares are scarce they are outside the scope of anything but a specialist work.

The history of the Goldsmiths of Ireland can
be traced back to pre-Norman times, and it
is certain that very much fine plate was made
between then and the fifteenth century when
the English Statute of 1423 was extended to
include Ireland, although there is little
evidence as to any effect it may have had. In
1555 there is a record of the Dublin Goldsmiths having to petition the City Council to
guarantee their status, as their precious charter had been 'accidentally burnt', and they
were anxious that with the loss of the charter
there might be a reciprocal loss in the
privileges they enjoyed under it. It was not
until 1557 that the worried goldsmiths were
granted their petition and allowed to operate
their guild within the law once again.

In 1605, as a result of both low standard
plate being found to be sold in Dublin and
the disappearance of a large volume of civic
plate which was suspected to have ended in

the melting pot of local goldsmiths, the City Council took action. The Council passed a resolution that each goldsmith should have his own mark and that all plate sold after 1st January 1606 should have first been assayed by 'the Mayor and Constables' of the city. It was also declared that the standard for plate should be the same as for coin (Sterling Standard), and that the mark of assay should be the figure of 'a lion, harp and a castle'.

King Charles I, in 1637, granted a charter of incorporation to the Dublin Goldsmiths under which there were provisions for the regular assay and marking of plate made within their jurisdiction. In order to comply with the conditions of the charter the mark of a crowned harp was adopted to signify that the plate had been assayed and was of acceptable quality. Date letters were also used in Dublin from 1638.

Duty was not introduced in Ireland until 1730, the figure of Hibernia being added to the other marks already in use to show that the duty had been paid, but it was not until 1752 that it was made illegal to sell plate without this mark. In 1784 a new Assay Office was opened at New Geneva, near Waterford, to deal with the trade brought by continental jewellers and watchmakers who had left the mainland of Europe because of their political or religious views. It was declared that the mark of this office should be different from those in use in Dublin. However, this was a very short lived venture, as the office closed down within three months of the legislation being passed for its opening, and it is unlikely that silver was ever marked there.

The Act of Union of 1801, like the Act of 1707 for Scotland, while leaving the laws relating to hall-marking as they were, made provision for them to be changed by the joint parliament if and when they deemed it necessary. This was the case in 1807, with the Plate Assay (Ireland) Act, which brought the conducting of the Dublin Office in line with its English counterparts and extended the duty which applied to England and Scotland to the Dublin goldsmiths. Thus, with the adding of the King's head, the figure of Hibernia was confirmed as a supplementary mark to the harp in identifying a piece as Dublin and of Sterling Standard, having completely lost its relevance as a duty mark.

The Government of Ireland Act 1920, declared all plate assayed in the Republic of Ireland after 1923 foreign from the point of view of the English Customs. So although most of the plate marked in Dublin can be labelled as British, that after 1923 must be regarded as Eirean.

There were a number of unofficial provincial centres in Ireland, especially in the eighteenth century, the two most important being Cork and Limerick.

THE MAKERS

THE MAKERS

Makers, their marks and history can be the most exciting and rewarding part of the study of silver, especially to the collector. A piece poses such problems as: Is it good quality? Was it made by the man whose mark it carries or in his workshop? Did the maker specialise in this particular aspect of the trade or was he a general smith? What class of patron was he working for—the nobility, aristocracy, wealthy untitled or the new middle class? These questions are not always very easy to answer, but in the case of the better and more fashionable smiths the history and development of their individual art and prosperity can be traced through their own work.

Probably the most famous English goldsmith is Paul de Lamerie who was, as his name indicates, a Huguenot immigrant. He was apprenticed to Pierre Platel, himself a fine workman who had been working in

England since about 1687, and after serving for seven years Lamerie entered his mark at Goldsmiths' Hall in 1712. The work of Paul de Lamerie is unmistakably Huguenot in the use of massive weight. Using the French styles of the period and adapting them to English taste, Lamerie was soon being patronised by the leaders of fashion and the nobility. His work was so far ahead of any of his contemporaries that in the 1730s when he was at the height of his career, he only had to introduce a new variation for it to be widely copied. One of the most famous techniques of his workshop resulted in the cast figures and handles, usually mythical and very often connected with the sea, which he felt was the nearest natural element to silver. Lamerie himself was certainly responsible for either the whole or part of nearly all the work produced in his workshop, and the undeniable quality of the finished products indicates that up to his death in 1751 he would accept nothing but the best. It is amusing to record that even he, with the huge revenue which he must have received, was tempted to use the duty-dodging techniques; in the Victoria and Albert Museum there is an ewer with the marks on the bottom let in for just this reason.

At the end of the seventeenth century came Anthony Nealme and Benjamin Pyne, both first class craftsmen. Nealme was one of the main exponents of the plain style which developed into what is called 'Queen Anne'. At the same time there was David Willaume senior, an exponent of the Chinese taste which was so fashionable in the last quarter of the century.

The middle years of the eighteenth century saw a trend toward specialist goldsmiths. The most prominent names were William Cafe who produced candlesticks; John Tuite who produced salvers and waiters, and Dorothy Mills, a specialist in salvers and the major craftswoman of the period. By 1760 the craft was expanding at such a fast rate that there was hardly a smith who did not run a workshop employing at least ten people, and a reduction in quality was the inevitable result of the over-demand for plate. Quality can be gauged by the weight; this is made easier in that a well-made

piece, regardless of the maker, will weigh
within ten per cent of the weight of a
piece of similar dimensions by another smith
of equal standing. An example of this is
cream jugs: a good one dated 1770 should
weigh around 4 oz Troy, while it is possible
to find jugs similar in appearance weighing
under 2 oz. Those makers who can generally
be relied upon to have made good quality
wares are listed in the tables.

There are very few people, even those
who know nothing about silver, who haven't
heard of Hester Bateman. The Bateman
family specialised in bottle tickets and sugar
tongs, both of which are of highly delightful
and original forms. However, the rest of the
wares produced in the workshop are generally run-of-the-mill standard and in all
probability Hester Bateman herself never
did more than oversee the workers. The
Bateman factory was at the peak of its popu-
larity during the height of the fashion for
neo-classical 'Adam' designs and, despite the
availability of better made pieces of the same
period, the appeal of the mark of a woman
caused both her and her workshop to be im-

mortalised in the history of the British gold-smiths above makers of superior quality.

After Hester Bateman, such craftsmen as Benjamin Smith and Paul Storr emerged. These two smiths were, after Paul de Lamerie, probably the best technical workers in silver ever. They were working in a period when it was fashionable to own and commission gigantic pieces of silver which, although heavy and massive, had to have a simplicity of line and a good utilitarian purpose. It was an age of grandeur when the rich colouring of silver gilt was better thought of than the clean white glow of silver; a time when Royal patronage could set a man up for life. Such was the case for Paul Storr and Rundell, Bridge and Rundell, the firm he worked for during the reign of George III. Over 100 people were employed in the workshops, all working on plate commissioned from Storr, all of which was marked with Storr's mark and most of which, excepting many of the spoons and forks, was of exceptional quality. Many of the smaller wares, especially the heavier amongst them, are of a lower standard and were probably fashioned by apprentices. Pieces by Paul Storr are found right through from 1790 to the 1830s.

The Victorian goldsmith in London was very much more of a foreman designer than his predecessor and the important makers became important manufacturers. However a few names stand out, most of which are as well known today as they must have been 100 years ago; names like Garrard and Mappin.

The goldsmiths of Chester were dominated by the family of Richardson, and between 1701 and 1787 there was always a smith called Richard Richardson working in the town. This spread of years covered three generations of the family which is almost as remarkable as the quality of the work they produced. Apart from the Richardsons, the only other Chester smith of any merit is John Sutters who specialised in the production of spoons and forks between 1835 and 1856. Sutters, like many of the makers whose marks are found at Chester, came from Liverpool. It is also worth looking for the mark of Matthew Boulton, a Birmingham manufacturer who was instrumental in the establishment of the Assay Office there in 1773, but who took some pieces for assay to Chester, usually to protect a new product from the pirating that could follow its exhibition to competitors who were goldsmith wardens at Birmingham.

Birmingham is very much Matthew Boulton and the amount of plate assayed there is almost a direct proportion to the fortunes of his factory in Soho. Boulton was a brilliant entrepreneur; he entered into partnership with James Watt to produce steam-driven engines and even produced coins for use in 1797. These coins were produced on a steam operated press and due to their size were called 'Cartwheel'. One of the Boulton apprentices, Edward Thomason, was to become one of the leading men in Birmingham. He became a diplomat and received honours from many European countries before returning to England to run his business, the wares produced by his workshop being equal to those of any of the provincial smiths. The other makers in Birmingham tended to specialise in small pieces—buttons, boxes, purses and seals etc.—and the most important of these are listed in the table.

Exeter had no outstanding smith and very little important plate appears to have been produced there. Sheffield also had a great many different makers, all of whom produced very much the same sort of product which was not of exceptional standard and often completely machine-made.

The goldsmiths of Newcastle were probably the most interesting of the eighteenth century provincial goldsmiths. The town specialised in mugs and tankards, and as there were a number of accomplished smiths there, the mugs were soon being sold throughout the country. John Langlands was probably the most prolific of the makers. He was usually in partnership and when he died his widow, Dorothy, kept the workshop open. Yet with the death of John Langlands the craft in Newcastle began to fade, and apart from Thomas Watson there were only four or five smiths working when the office was closed in 1884.

York, as already mentioned, was the exception to all the other Assay towns, for when re-opened in 1776 there was only one main workshop in the city—the partnership of John Hampston and John Prince—and some watchmakers. All the way through the next 80 years it was only this workshop which kept the office open.

The study of provincial makers is interesting, not only because of their scarcity, but because the field is so large that it is possible, with a little bit of luck and perseverance, to obtain original material relating to the goldsmiths themselves, their workshops, debts, misdeeds and achievements.

Interior of a silversmith's workshop

TABLES OF MAKERS' MARKS

TABLES OF MAKERS' MARKS

LONDON
1702–1720

AS	Thomas Ash	R ⎰	David and
BU	Thomas Burridge	D.H ⎱ H	Robert Hennell
FO	Thomas Folkingham	SM	Samuel Meriton
NE	Antony Nealme	DM	Dorothy Mills
PL	Pierre Platel	PP	Pere Pilleau
Py	Benjamin Pyne	W ⎰ W.S ⎱ P	William Shaw and William Priest
WI	David Willaume	S ⎰ GS ⎱ S	George and S. Smith

1720–1770

EA	Edward Aldridge	RS	Robert Swanson
WC	William Cafe	T & W	Turner and Williams
T ⎰ WC⎱ C	Thomas and William Chawner		
BC	Benjamin Cooper		
FC	Francis Crump		**1770–1820**
DPW	Dobson, Prior, and Williams	HB	Hester Bateman
EF	Edward Feline	PB ⎰ AB ⎱	Peter and Ann Bateman
		RC	Richard Crossly

53

WE WF {	William Eley and William Fearn	GS WF {	George Smith and William Fearn
WE WF WC {	William Eley, William Fearn and William Chawner	PS	Paul Storr
		MS ES {	Mary and Elizabeth Sumner
JƐ	John Emes	WS	William Sumner
RE EB {	Rebecca Emes and Edward Barnard	GW	George Wintle
		1820–1850	
RG	Robert Garrard	GA	George Adams
SH	Samuel Hennel	JA IA {	J & J Aldous
RM RC {	Robert Makepeace and Richard Carter	MC	Mary Chawner
		RH	Robert Hennell
TN	Thomas Northcote	HH	Hyam Hyams
TO	Thomas Olliphant	IL HL {	John, Henry and Charles
WP	William Pitts	CL	Lias
RR	Robert Rutland	AS JS {	Adey, Joshua and Albert
IS	John Scholfield	AS	Savory
DS RS {	David Smith and Robert Sharpe	JS AS {	Joshua and Albert Savory
		WRS	W. R. Smiley
		PS	Paul Storr

PROVINCIAL MAKERS' MARKS

BIRMINGHAM

1773–1820

MB	Matthew Boulton
SP	Samuel Pemberton
IT	Joseph Taylor
TW	Thomas Willmore
ML	Matthew Linwood
WP	William Pugh
ET	Edward Thomason
JW	Joseph Willmore

1820–1850

NM	Nathanial Mills
ES	Edward Smith
GU	George Unite
ET	Edward Thomason
JW	Joseph Willmore
L & Co.	John Lawrence and Co.
P & T	William Postan and George Tye
T & P	Joseph Taylor & John Perry

CHESTER

1700-1720

Ma	Thomas Maddock
Ri	Richard Richardson
Ro	Thomas Robinson
Du	Bartholomew Duke

1720-1770

TM	Thomas Maddock
BP	Benjamin Pemberton
RP	Richard Pike
RR	Richard Richardson
WR	William Richardson

1770-1830

JA	John Adamson
MB	Matthew Boulton
RB	Robert Bowers
WH	William Hull
GL	George Lowe
EM	Edward Maddock
WP	William Pugh
RR	Richard Richardson
GW	George Walker
IW	Joseph Walley

1830-1870

FB	Francis Butt
IL { TL {	John & Thomas Lowe
JL	John Lowe
RL	Robert Lowe
GR	George Roberts
IR	John Richards

EXETER

1701–1720

AR	Peter Arno	JH	Joseph Hicks
SA	Thomas Salter	SL	Simon Lery
		JO	John Osmont
SL	Daniel Slade	IP	Isaac Parkin

1720–1770

TB	Thomas Blake	WP	William Pearse
DC	Daniel Coleman	GT	George Turner
WP	William Parry	WW	William West (senior and junior)

TS	Thomas Sampson

1830–1882

RS	Richard Sams	JO	John Osmont
		IP	Isaac Parkin
JS	James Strong	WP	William Pope
		WRS	W. R. Sobey

1770–1830

GF	George Ferris (son of Richard)	SOBEY	W. R. Sobey
		JS	John Stone
		TS	Thomas Stone
RF	Richard Ferris	JW	James Williams

NEWCASTLE

1702–1720

Ki	James Kirkup	DL	Dorothy Langlands
LA	John Langwith	IL	John Langlands
YO	John Younghusband	GM	George Murray
Ra	John Ramsay	AR	Anne Robertson

1720–1790

DC	David Crawford	IR	John Robertson
IC	Isaac Cookson	RS	Robert Scott
JG	John Goodriche	IW	John Walton
IK	James Kirkup	TW	Thomas Watson
JL	John Langlands		

IL ⎱ John Langlands and
IR ⎰ John Robertson

RM	Robert Makepeace
TP	Thomas Partis
CR	Christian Reid
IS	John Stoddart

1790–1830

MA	Mary Ashworth (of Durham)

1830–1883

WL	William Lister

WL ⎫
CL ⎬ Lister and Sons
WL ⎭

DR	David Reid
TS	Thomas Sewill
IW	John Walton
TW	Thomas Watson

YORK
1776–1856

IH IP	John Hampston John Prince 1798		JB & Co	James Barber & Co 1825
HP & C	John Hampston John Prince Robert Cattle 1802		BC & N	James Barber George Cattle William North 1828
P & C	John Prince Robert Cattle 1808		J B G C W N	James Barber George Cattle William North 1837
RC J B	Robert Cattle James Barber 1812			
J B WW	James Barker William Whitwell 1821		J B W N	James Barber William North 1847
			JB	James Barber 1856

SHEFFIELD

1773–1820

GA & Co	George Ashforth & Co
MF RC	Fenton Creswick & Co
WD	William Damant
IG & Co	John Green
IL	John Law
TL	Thomas Law
TL DL	Thomas & Daniel Leader
RM	Richard Marden & Co
RM & Co	Richard Mark and Co
IP & W	John Parsons and Co
NS & W	Nathanial Smith & Co
IW & Co	John Winter and Co
ITY & Co	J. T. Younge and Co

1820–1870

JB	James Burbury
MH & Co	Martin Hall and Co
RM EH	Martin Hall and Co
HE & Co	Hawksworth Eyre and Co
H & H	Howard & Hawksworth
HW & Co	Henry Wilkinson and Co

60

EDINBURGH

1700–1759

WG	William Ged	JD	James Douglas
WG	William Gilchrist	AH	Alexander Henderson
IK	James Ker		
RK	Robert Ker	PR	Patrick Robertson
EL	Edward Livingstone	WR	William Robertson
EO	Edward Oliphant	AZ	Alexander Zeigler
LO	Lawrence Oliphant	IZ	John Zeigler
IR	John Rollo		
GS	George Scott		

1800–1850

WS	Walter Scott	AH	Alexander Henderson
AU	Archibald Ure	JMc	J. McKay
		J & WM	James and William Marshall

1760–1800

RB	Robert Bowman	PS	Peter Sutherland
GC	George Christie	AZ	Alexander Zeigler
RC	Robert Clark	E & Co	Elder and Co
ID	James Dempster		

61

GLASGOW

1819–1850

PA	Peter Arthur
JC	James Crichton
RD	Robert Duncan
RG	Robert Gray
& S	and Son
D McD	David McDonald
AM	Alexander Mitchell
JM	John Mitchell
WP	William Parkins

DUBLIN

1700–1730
RC	Robert Calderwood
IC	John Cuthbert
IH	John Hamilton
DK	David King
HM	Henry Matthews
TP	Thomas Parker

1730–1770
IC	John Christie
WC	William Currie
JD	James Douglas
DK	David King
TK	Thomas Kinslea
AL	Anthony Lefebure
WT	William Townsend

1770–1820
IB	John Buckton
WC	William Cummins
DE	Daniel Egan
MK	Michael Keating
TK	Thomas Kinslea
SN	Samuel Neville
J.P	John Pittar
JP	John Power
WR	William Rose
RS	Richard Sawyer
IS	James Scott
MW	Matthew West

1820–1850
GA	George Alcock
IB	John Buckton
WL	William Lawson
PM	P. Moore
EP	Edward Power
PW	Peter Walsh

TABLES OF DATE LETTERS

TABLE OF MARKS ON LONDON PLATE

A	1678	1697	1716	1736	1756	1776	1796	1816	1836	1856
B	1679	1697	1717	1737	1757	1777	1797	1817	★37	1857
C	1680	1698	1718	1738	1758	1778	1798	1818	1838	1858
D	1681	1699	★19	★39	1759	1779	1799	1819	1839	1859
E	1682	1700	1720	1740	1760	1780	1800	1820	1840	1860
F	1863	1701	1721	1741	1761	1781	1801	★21	1841	1861
G	1684	1702	1722	1742	1762	1782	1802	1822	1842	1862
H	1685	1703	1723	1743	1763	1783	1803	1823	1843	1863
I	1686	1704	1724	1744	1764	★84	1804	1824	1844	1864
K	1687	1705	1725	1745	1765	★85	1805	1825	1845	1865
L	1688	1706	1726	1746	1766	★86	1806	1826	1846	1866
M	1689	1707	1727	1747	1767	1787	1807	1827	1847	1867
N	1690	1708	1728	1748	1768	1788	1808	1828	1848	1868
O	1691	1709	1729	1749	1769	1789	1809	1929	1849	1869
P	1692	1710	1730	1750	1770	1790	1810	1830	1850	1870
Q	1693	1711	1731	1751	1771	1791	1811	1831	1851	1871
R	1694	1712	1732	1752	1772	1792	1812	1832	1852	1872
S	1695	1713	1733	1753	1773	1793	1813	1833	1853	1873
T	1696	1714	1734	1754	1774	1794	1814	1834	1854	1874
U	——	1715	1735	1755	1775	1795	1815	1835	1855	1875

Throughout the tables the date letters have been printed black on white (not white on black as in the shields) for ease of identification.

A	1876	1896	1916	1936	1956
B	1877	1897	1917	1937	1957
C	1878	1898	1918	1938	1958
D	1879	1899	1919	1939	1959
E	1880	1900	1920	1940	1960
F	1881	1901	1921	1941	1961
G	1882	1902	1922	1942	1962
H	1883	1903	1923	1943	1963
I	1884	1904	1924	1944	1964
K	1885	1905	1925	1945	1965
L	1886	1906	1926	1946	1966
M	1887	1907	1927	1947	1967
N	1888	1908	1928	1948	1968
O	1889	1909	1929	1949	1969
P	1890	1910	1930	1950	1970
Q	1891	1911	1931	1951	
R	1892	1912	1932	1952	
S	1893	1913	1933	1953	
T	1894	1914	1934	1954	
U	1895	1915	1935	1955	

1719 Brittania Standard becomes voluntary and sterling marks are re-introduced.

1784–6 Octagonal intaglio King's Head duty mark used.

1786–1837 Oval King's Head duty mark used but in 1797 it can be found in silhouette.

1821 Leopard's Head becomes uncrowned.

1837–90 Queen's Head duty mark used.

1935 King and Queen's Head stamped to celebrate Silver Jubilee of George V.

A	1773	1798	1824	1849	1875	1900	1925	1950
B	1774	1799	1825	1850	1876	1901	1926	1951
C	1775	1880	1826	1851	1877	1902	1927	1952
D	1766	1801	1827	1852	1878	1903	1928	1953
E	1777	1802	1828	1853	1879	1904	1929	1954
F	1778	1803	1829	1854	1880	1905	1930	1955
G	1779	1804	1830	1855	1881	1906	1931	1956
H	1780	1805	1831	1856	1882	1907	1932	1957
I	1781	1806	1832	1857	1883	1908		
J	—	1807	—	1858	—		1933	1958
K	1782	1808	1833	1859	1884	1909	1934	1959
L	1783	1809	1834	1860	1885	1910	1935	1960
M	★84	1810	1835	1861	1886	1911	1936	1961
N	1785	1811	1836	1862	1887	1912	1937	1962
O	★86	★12	1837	1863	1888	1913	1938	1963
P	1787	1813	★38	1864	1899	1914	1939	1964
Q	1788	1814	1839	1865	1890	1915	1940	1965
R	1789	1815	1840	1866	1891	1916	1941	1966
S	1790	1816	1841	1867	1892	1917	1942	1967
T	1791	1817	1842	1868	1893	1918	1943	1968
U	1792	1818	1843	1869	1894	1919	1944	1969
V	1793	1819	1844	1870	1895	1920	1945	1970
W	1794	1820	1845	1871	1896	1921	1946	
X	1795	1821	1846	1872	1897	1922	1947	
Y	1796	1822	1847	1873	1898	1923	1948	
Z	1797†	1823	1848	1874	1899	1924	1949	

1784–5 Octagonal intaglio King's Head duty mark used.

1785–97 Oval King's Head duty mark used.

1797 Double duty mark sometimes used.

1797–1833 Oval or silhouette King's Head duty mark used.

1833 William IV Head used in Oval.

1838 Queen Victoria's Head introduced until removal of duty in 1890.

1935 King and Queen's Head stamped to celebrate Silver Jubilee of George V.

TABLE OF MARKS ON CHESTER PLATE

A	1701	1726	1751	1776	1797	1818	1839	1864	1884	1901
B	1702	1727	1752	1777	1798	1819	1840	1865	1885	1902
C	1703	1728	1753	1778	1799	1820	1841	1866	1886	1903
D	1704	1729	1754	1779	1800	1821/2	1842	1867	1887	1904
E	1705	1730	1755	1780	★01	★23	1843	1868	1888	1905
F	1706	1731	1756	1781	1802	1824	1844	1869	1889	1906
G	1707	1732	G 57	1782	1803	1825	1845	1870	1890	1907
H	1708	1733	1758	1783	1804	1826	1846	1871	1891	1908
I	1709	1734	1759	★84	1805	1827	1847	1872	1892	1909
J										
K	1710	1735	1760	1785	1806	1828	1848	1873	1893	1910
L	1711	1736	1761	★86	1807	1829	1849	1874	1894	1911
M	1712	1737	1762	1787	1808	1830	1850	1875	1895	1912
N	1713	1738	1763	1788	1809	1831	1851	1876	1896	1913
O	1714	1739	1764	1789	1810	1832	1852	1877	1897	1914
P	1715	1740	P 65	1790	1811	1833	1853	1878	1898	1915
Q	1716	1741	Q 66	1791	1812	1834.	1854	1879	1899	1916
R	1717	1742	R 67	1792	1813	★35	1855	1880	1900	1917
S	1718	1743	1768	1793	1814	1836	1856	1881	——	1918
T	★19	1744	1769	1794	1815	1837	1857	1882	——	1919
U	1720	1745	U 70	1795	1816	1838	1858	1883	——	1920
V	1721	1746	V 71	1796	1817	——	1859	——	——	1921
W	1722	1747	W 72	——	——	——	1860	——	——	1922
X	1723	1748	X 73	——	——	——	1861	——	——	1923
Y	1724	1749	Y 74	——	——	——	1862	——	——	1924
Z	1725	1750	(1775)	——	——	——	1863	——	——	1925

A	1926	1951	**1719** Brittania Standard becomes voluntary and sterling marks are re-introduced.
B	1927	1952	
C	1928	1953	
D	1929	1954	
E	1930	1955	
F	1931	1956	**1767–75** Date letter marks in serated punch.
G	1932	1957	
H	1933	1958	
I	1934	——	
J	——	1959	**1779** New town mark introduced.
K	1935	1960	
L	1936	1961	**1784–6** Octagonal intaglio King's Head duty mark used.
M	1937	1962	
N	1938		
O	1939		**1786–1835** Normally silhouette King's Head duty mark used although it is sometimes found in an oval.
P	1940		
Q	1941		
R	1942		
S	1943		
T	1944		
U	1945		
V	1946		**1835–40** Either silhouette or oval King's Head duty mark used.
W	1947		
X	1948		
Y	1949		
Z	1950		**1840–90** Oval Queen's Head duty mark used.

TABLE OF MARKS ON EXETER PLATE

A	1701	1725	1749	1773	1797	1817	1837	1857	1877
B	1702	1726	1750	1774	1798	1818	1838	1858	1878
C	1703	1727	1751	1775	1799	1819	1839	1859	1879
D	1704	1728	1752	1776	1800	1820	1840	1860	1880
E	1705	1729	1753	1777	1801	1821	1841	1861	1881
F	1706	1730	1754	1778	1802	1822	1842	1862	1882
G	1707	1731	1755	1779	1803	1823	★43	1863	
H	1708	1732	1756	1780	1804	1824	1844	1864	
I	1709	1733	1757	1781/2	1805	1825	1845	1865	
K	1710	1734	1758	1783	1806	1826	1846	1866	
L	1711	1735	1759	★84	1807	1827	1847	1867	
M	1712	1736	1760	1785	1808	1828	1848	1868	
N	1713	1737	1761	★86	1809	1829	1849	1869	
O	1714	1738	1762	1787	1810	1830	1850	1870	
P	1715	1739	1763	1788	1811	1831	1851	1871	
Q	1716	1740	1764	q 89	1812	1832	1852	1872	
R	1717	1741	1765	r 90	1813	1833	1853	1873	
S	1718	1742	1766	f 91	1814	★34	1854	1874	
T	1719	1743	1767	t 92	1815	1835	1855	1875	
T U	—	1744	1768	u 93	1816	1836	1856	1876	
U	1720								
W	★21	1745	1769	1794					
X	1722	1746	1770	1795	—	—	—	—	
Y	1723	1747	1771	1796	—	—	—	—	
Z	1724	1748	1772	—	—	—	—	—	

1721 Britannia
Standard becomes
voluntary and
sterling marks are
re-introduced.
1784–6 Octagonal
intaglio King's Head
duty mark used.
1886–97 Oval King's
Head duty mark used.
1797–1816 Either
oval or silhouette
King's Head duty
mark used.
1816–38 Oval
King's Head duty
mark used.
1833 William IV
Head introduced.
1838–82 Oval
Queen's Head duty
mark used.

A	1721	1740	1759	1791	1815	1839	1864
B	1722	1741	1760/8	1792	1816	1840	1865
C	1723	1742	1769	1793	1817	★41	1866
D	1724	1743	1770	1794	1818	1842	1867
E	1725	1744	1771	1795	1819	1843	1868
F	1726	1745	1772	1796	1820	1844	1869
G	★27	1746	1773	★97	★21	1845	1870
H	1728	1747	1774	1798	1822	★46	1871
I	1729	1748	1775	1799	1823	1847	1872
J	——	——	——	——	——	1848	——
K	1730	1749	1776	1800	1824	1849	1873
L	1731	1750	1777	1801	1825	1850	1874
M	1732	1751	1778	1802	1826	1851	1875
N	1733	1752	1779	1803	1827	1852	1876
O	1734	1753	1780	1804	1828	1853	1877
P	1735	1754	1781	1805	1829	1854	1878
Q	1736	1755	1782	1806	1830	1855	1879
R	1737	1756	1783	1807	1831	1856	1880
S	1738	★57	★84	1808	1832	1857	1881
T	1739	(1758)	1785	1809	1833	1858	1882
U	——	——	★86	1810	1834	1859	1883
W	——	——	1787	1811	1835	1860	
X	——	——	1788	1812	1836	1861	
Y	——	——	1789	1813	1837	1862	
Z	——	——	1790	1814	1838	1863	

1721–28 Sterling Standard mark sometimes faces to the right instead of the left.

*1733–90 Date letters are roman capitals and NOT italics.

1784–5 Octagonal intaglio King's Head duty mark used.

1786–96 Oval King's Head duty mark used.

1797–1820 Silhouette King's Head duty mark used.

1821–32 Oval King's Head duty mark used.

1832–42 Oval William IV King's Head duty mark used.

1840–84 Oval Queen's Head duty mark used.

A	1776	1787	1812	1837
B	1777	1788	1813	1838
C	1778	1789	1814	1839
D	1779	1790	1815	★40
E	1780	1791	1816	1841
F	1781	1792	1817	1842
G	1782	1793	1818	1843
H	1783	1794	1819	1844
I	——	1795	1820	1845
J	★84	1795	——	
K	1785	1796	1821	1846
L	★86	1797	1822	1847
M	——	1798	1823	1848
N	——	1799	1824	1849
O	——	1800	1825	1850
P	——	1801	1826	1851
Q	——	1802	1827	1852
R	——	1803	1828	1853
S	——	1804	1829	1854
T	——	1805	1830	1855
U	——	1806	1831	
V	——	1807	1832	1856
W	——	1808	1833	
X	——	1809	1834	
Y	——	1810	1835	
Z	——	1811	1836	

1784–5 Octagonal King's Head duty mark used.

1785–96 Oval King's Head duty mark used.

1796–1825 Silhouette King's Head duty mark used.

1825–39 Both oval and silhouette King's Head duty mark used.

From **1839** Queen's Head in oval.

A	1779	1806	1824	1844	1868	1893	1918	1943	1968
B	1783	1805	1825	1845	1869	1894	1919	1944	1969
C	1780	1811	1826	1846	1870	1895	1920	1945	1970
D	1781	1812	1827	1847	1871	1896	1921	1946	
E	1773	1799	1828	1848	1872	1897	1922	1947	
F	1774	1803	1829	1849	1873	1898	1923	1948	
G	1782	1804	1830	1850	1874	1899	1924	1949	
N	1777	1801	1831	1851	1875	1900	1925	1950	
I	★84	1818	——	1852	——	1901	1926	1951	
J	——	——	——	——	1876	——	——	——	
K	★86	1809	1832	1853	1877	1902	1927	1952	
L	1790	1810	1833	1854	1878	1903	1928	1953	
M	1789/94	1802	★34	1855	1879	1904	1929	1954	
N	1775	1800	——	1856	1880	1905	1930	1955	
O	1793	1815	——	1857	1881	1906	1931	1956	
P	1791	1808	1835	1858	1882	1907	1932	1957	
Q	1795	1820	1836	——	1883	1908	1933	1958	
R	1776	1813	1837	1859	1884	1909	1934	1959	
S	1778	1807	1838	1860	1885	1910	1935	1960	
T	1787	1816	1839	1861	1886	1911	1936	1961	
U	1792	1823	1840	1862	1887	1912	1937	1962	
V	1798	1819	1841	1863	1888	1913	1938	1963	
W	1788	1814	——	1864	1889	1914	1939	1964	
X	1797†	1817	1842	1865	1890	1915	1940	1965	
Y	1785	1821	——	1866	1891	1916	1941	1966	
Z	1796	1822	1843	1867	1892	1917	1942	1967	

From the opening in
1773 the town marks
and date letter were
amalgamated on small
pieces of silver to
prevent unnecessary
damage.
1784–6 Octagonal
intaglio King's Head
duty mark used.
1786–96 Oval King's
Head duty mark used.
1797 Double duty
mark sometimes used.
1796–1824 Silhouette
King's Head duty
mark used.
1835 William IV
Head introduced.
1824–40 Oval King's
Head duty mark used.

TABLE OF MARKS ON EDINBURGH PLATE

A	1705	1730	1755	1780	1806	1832	1857	1882	1906
B	1706	1731	1756	1781	1807	1833	1858	1883	1907
C	★07	1732	1757	1782	1808	1834	1859	1884	1908
D	1708	1733	1758	1783	1809	1835	1860	1885	1909
E	1709	1734	★59	★84	1810	1836	1861	1886	1910
F	1710	1735	1760	1785	1811	1837	1862	1887	1911
G	1711	1736	1761	★86/7	1812	1838	1863	1888	1912
H	1712	1737	1762	1788	1813	1839	1864	1889	1913
I	1713	1738	1763	1789	1814	1840	1865	1890	1914
J				1789	1815				
K	1714	1739	1764	1790	1816	★41	1866	1891	1915
L	1715	★40	1765	1791	1817	1842	1867	1892	1916
M	1716	1741	1766	1792	1818	1843	1868	1893	1917
N	1717	★42	1767	1793	1819	1844	1869	1894	1918
O	1718	1743	1768	1794	1820	1845	1870	1895	1919
P	1719	★44	1769	1795	1821	1846	1871	1896	1920
Q	1720	1745	1770	1796	1822	1847	1872	1897	1921
R	1721	1746	1771	★97	★23	1848	1873	1898	1922
S	1722	1747	1772	1798	★24	1849	1874	1899	1923
T	1723	1748	1773	1799	1825	1850	1875	1900	1924
U	1724	1749	1774	1800	1826	1851	1876	1901	1925
V	1725	1750	1775	1801	1827	1852	1877	1901	1926
W	1726	1751	—	1802	1828	1853	1878	1902	1927
X	1727	1752	1776	1803	1829	1854	1879	1903	1928
Y	1728	1753	1777	1804	1830	1855	1880	1904	1929
Z	1729	1754	1778	1805	1831	1856	1881	1905	1930

A	1931	1956
B	1932	1957
C	1933	1958
D	1934	1959
E	1935	1960
F	1936	1961
G	1937	1962
H	1938	1963
I	1939	1964
J	—	—
K	1940	1965
L	1941	1966
M	1942	1967
N	1943	1968
O	1944	1969
P	1945	1970
Q	1946	
R	1947	
S	1948	
T	1949	
U	1950	
V	1951	
W	1952	
X	1953	
Y	1954	
Z	1955	

1759 Thistle mark introduced.

1784–6 Octagonal intaglio King's Head duty mark used.

1786–96 Oval King's Head duty mark used.

1796–1823 Silhouette King's Head duty mark used.

1786–1826 Various forms of Castles used.

1823–40 Oval King's Head duty mark used.

1840–90 Oval Queen's Head duty mark used.

TABLE OF MARKS ON GLASGOW PLATE

A	1819	1845	1871	1897	1923	1949
B	1820	1846	1872	1898	1924	1950
C	1821	1847	1873	1899	1925	1951
D	1822	1848	1874	1900	1926	1952
E	1823	1849	1875	1901	1927	1953
F	1824	1850	1876	1902	1928	1954
G	1825	1851	1877	1903	1929	1955
H	1826	1852	1878	1904	1930	1956
I	1827	1853	1879	1905	1931	1957
J	1828	1854	1880	1906	1932	——
K	1829	1855	1881	1907	1933	——
L	1830	1856	1882	1908	1934	1958
M	1831	1857	1883	1909	1935	1959
N	1832	1858	1884	1910	1936	1960
O	1833	1859	1885	1911	1937	1961
P	1834	1860	1886	1912	1938	1962
Q	1835	1861	1887	1913	1939	1963
R	1836	1862	1888	★14	1940	
S	1837	1863	1889	1915	1941	
T	1838	1864	1890	1916	1942	
U	1839	1865	1891	1917	1943	
V	★40	1866	1892	1918	1944	
W	1841	1867	1893	1919	1945	
X	1842	1868	1894	1920	1946	
Y	1843	1869	1895	1921	1947	
Z	1844	1870	1896	1922	1948	

1841–90 Oval
Queen's Head duty
mark used.

TABLE OF MARKS ON DUBLIN PLATE

A	1720	1747	1773	1797	1821	1846	1871	1896	1916
B	1721	1748	1774	1798	1822	1847	1872	1897	1917
C	1722	1749	1775	1799	1823	1848	1873	1898	1918
D	1723	1750	D 76	1800	1824	1849	1874	1899	1919
E	1724	1751	E 77	1801	1825	1850	1875	1900	1920
F	1725	1752	F 78	1802	1826	1851	1876	1901	1921
G	1726	1753	G 79	1803	1827	1852	1877	1902	1922
H	1727	1754	H 80	1804	1828	1853	1878	1903	
I	1728	1757	I 81	1805	1829		1879	1904	
J	—	—	—	—	—	1854	—	—	
K	1729	1758	K 72	1906	1830	1855	1880	1905	
L	1730/1†	1759	L 83	1807	1831	1856	1881	1906	
M	1732	1760	M84	1808	1832	1857	1882	1907	
N	1733	1761	1785	★09	1833	1858	1883	1908	
O	1734	1762	1786	1810	1834	1859	1884	1909	
P	1735	1763	★87	1811	1835	1860	1885	1910	
Q	1736	1764	1788	1812	1836	1861	1886	1911	
R	1737	1765	1789	1813	1837	1862	1887	1912	
S	1738	1766	1790	1814	1838	1863	1888	1913	
T	1739	1767	1791	1815	1839	★64	1889	1914	
U	1740	1768	1792	1816	1840	1865	1890	1915	
U	—	—	—	—	1841	1866	1891	—	
W	1741/2	1769	1793	1817	1842	1867	1892	—	
X	1743/4	1770	★94	1818	1843	1868	1893	—	
Y	1745	1771	1795	1819	1844	1869	1894	—	
Y	1745	1771	1795	1819	1844	1869	1894	—	
Z	1746	1772	1796	1820	1845	1870	1895	—	

From **1730** Figure
of Hibernia used as
duty mark.

For details of various
Harps and Hibernias
used between **1730**
and **1772** refer to the
booklet *Hall-marks
On Dublin Silver*
published by the
National Museum of
Ireland.

1807–9 Rectangular
King's Head duty
mark used.

1809–21 King's
Head duty mark in
shield used.

1821–46 Many
different shields used
for all symbols, but
these can be
recognised by
eliminating the other
series first.

1838–90 Oval
Queen's Head duty
mark used.

READING HALL-MARKS

READING HALL-MARKS

Reading silver marks is an acquired art, the more you do the easier it becomes. It is quite unnecessary to sit down and try to learn the various date-letter cycles unless really understanding the intricacies and differences between parallel series in different towns. Perhaps the easiest way to learn to read hall-marks is to start with a known quantity. Very much more plate was assayed in London than elsewhere, and therefore the chances of finding a London mark are much better than, for example, finding an Exeter one. All London marks before 1780 are quite large punches with very clear pictures of the symbols represented in high relief. They will be found near the bowl of a spoon on the back of the stem (known as bottom-marked), and on jugs and vessels with handles either near the handle or on the bottom, and if there is no handle probably on the bottom. Sometimes, because the marks were in a vulnerable position they became worn and are now difficult to read. In order to read the mark more easily blow heavily on the piece near the mark. This will cause condensation on the cold metal, and while the surface is matt with the condensation, any small relief will show up more clearly.

The first step to identification is to look for a town mark: if none is apparent the first choice must be London. Next it is the turn of the variable date letter to be subjected to scrutiny. Is it a capital or small letter? What sort of script is the letter? What sort of shield is the letter in? Now, and *only* now is it time to refer to the table.—Is there a similar series, does it agree? If the mark in question has a king's head duty mark, does the mark in the series in question look similar? Is the lion in the same shield? If all things agree, and only *if*, then may an attribution be made. Under no circumstances can a mark which does not agree be forced into an attribution.

After 1780 the London marks are usually in a straight horizontal line, all the marks except the maker's mark being placed on a piece at once, rather than one at a time: the exception to this is the octagonal intaglio king's head duty mark which was used with the re-introduction of duty in 1784. On spoons and forks the marks are now found at the top of the back of the stem, while items such as cream jugs are sometimes marked under the lip or around the base. Teapots are the exception to this rule, and are generally marked on the bottom with the four main marks arranged around the maker's mark in the centre.

All the various provincial towns used the town mark until 1773, which makes exact attribution very much easier, but simple rules must still be followed. Even if the castle does look like Edinburgh, if the piece is marked with a lion it *must* be English, and in all probability it will be Exeter. After 1773 it becomes very much more difficult because often, especially on small pieces, the town mark is left off. The technique with these pieces is to work on a process of elimination, remembering that the chances are that the mark is a London one, and once again that after 1780 London marks without the town mark are in a straight line, the shield for the date letter rounded. In Exeter, however, the shields are either exactly rectangular with the king's head duty mark struck separately, or else there is only a lion in an oval shield with a stippled background and the maker's mark (this lion mark, which is not in the tables, was used from 1797 until 1808). The Chester equivalent has a very coarse lion with the corners of the shield cut or later a very narrow shield, but Georgian Chester is very scarce.

After 1821, both Exeter and London introduced the town mark on even the smallest of items, such as bottle tickets. Newcastle leaves off the date letter in preference to the town mark, while it is unusual to find a Birmingham piece without a full mark, even if it is disguised. Vinaigrettes—small boxes fitted with a grille under which is a sponge which would have been soaked in smelling salts—offer good examples of this type of marking. Often these are only marked on the lid with the town mark and the king's head duty mark with the maker's mark, while the grille is marked with a lion, and the base is marked with the lion, date letter and maker's mark again. Sheffield, because of the many very small pieces brought for assay, used the clever device of amalgamating the town mark and the variable date letter in one punch; sometimes the crown is upside down to differentiate from a previous series.

York has not been mentioned so far. This town presents a very difficult problem even for people who have been handling silver for a considerable amount of time. After the re-opening of the office in 1776 the marks used were similar in appearance to those in use in London, and it is the exception rather than the rule for the town mark to be used. The method of attribution must, therefore, be more complicated than with the other provincial towns. One method is through the makers' marks, which are listed before the date tables. Other clues are that the punches are individually struck and the detail of the punches is very poor.

It is important to remember that there is only one correct attribution regardless of how many alternatives there appear to be, and that can be reached only by practical reasoning. It is impossible for a piece with a king's head duty mark to be before 1784 however similar the marks look to an earlier cycle. Likewise, if it has a queen's head duty mark it cannot be before 1837, as that was the year of Queen Victoria's accession.

COLLECTING

COLLECTING

Collecting silver sounds like an expensive hobby and with the publicity that is given to fluctuations of price it seems insecure. But why be avaricious? Who needs to collect coffee pots which all look very much alike at £2,000 each, when they can have a very fine collection of, say, sugar tongs at £5 each if they obey some very simple rules and are prepared to wait for good opportunities?

The first question is what to collect? The choice should be governed by both budget and taste. It is nice to be able to add to the collection at regular intervals but it is not going to help the collection if it is not much loved.

Once the choice is made, but before buying anything, find out something about the history and development of the subject. This is best done by visiting and talking to local antique dealers, looking at any pieces they might have and the price they are asking for them, and from these two factors deciding why one is more expensive than another. Try a visit to a local auction room, where you will almost certainly see some pieces sold, and note how much they fetch. Compare the prices in auction with the prices in the shops, but remember that the dealer has to buy somewhere and only makes his living out of the difference between what he pays and what he can sell for.

Go to the library, and if there is not a book exclusively on your chosen subject, try the indexes of the books on silver on the shelf. There are very few subjects which have been given solo treatment but there will probably be chapters of relevant material.

Now is the time to start the collection. To begin with buy only from reputable dealers. Don't be frightened to pay a little more for something that is obviously special and avoid buying just because it appears to be cheap; more often than not an apparently cheap buy is a bad buy. The thing to go for is quality because, regardless of market variations, it is the good quality pieces which both appreciate fastest and hold their value in a time of deflation.

Do not buy any piece that has been mended. Mends are usually quite apparent if they are looked for, as with the duty-dodging of the early eighteenth century; the goldsmith had to use silver-solder to make his mend and when the silver is tested by blowing on it the solder shows brown. There are weak points on nearly every type of piece made of silver. In the case of cream jugs it is the join on the handle which often gets torn and needs to be mended. With tea-pots it is the spout or lid that often needs attention or there may be bruising around the base where it has been dropped. Salvers lose feet, beermugs have handle trouble, salt cellars often have very rubbed marks which detract from their value, spoons become torn at the bowl, forks have their prongs levelled off when they are worn, sugar-tongs bend and break near the top (look inside the bow), mustard-pots get new lids while muffineers split round the middle and get new tops which have different marks from the bases. These are just a few of the hazards which must be looked out for. They are all quite common and can be found without looking very far. One of the greatest pitfalls facing the collector of items such as those listed above is the fashion in the middle of the last century for highly decorated silver. In order to impress friends and neighbours vast amounts of plain Georgian silver was sent to be altered by having swags of flowers chased onto it. This method of decoration by placing a steel model on the inside of a piece, heating the silver till soft and then hammering it onto the steel, bringing the decoration through the silver, cuts the value of the piece by at least half.

Much fun can be obtained by collecting the work of just one smith, because as each piece is added the collector gets a better and better insight into the mind of the man himself, his peak years, his favourite patterns and what, if anything, he specialised in. With some of the Birmingham makers of the early nineteenth century this sort of collection can be particularly rewarding, as the variety of the wares produced, especially by such makers as Samuel Pemberton, Joseph

Willmore and Joseph Taylor was remarkably diverse. Other ideas are to collect just the wares of one town, say, Exeter. This form of collection will prove fascinating as the whims of the individual makers will emerge alongside local specialities.

Collecting by date letter is another possibility which can be very rewarding; either collecting pieces which have all been made in the same year and comparing the various styles and techniques used by the different makers in a particular year, or collecting by years—trying to have a piece representing each year in a series. It is best to collect the same item all the way through so that the development of the piece can be traced and the better makers identified by the easy comparison with the other pieces in the collection.

These are just a few thoughts on how to go about forming a collection of some aesthetic importance, together with a reasonable investment potential. It is vital to a collection that it bears the stamp of its owner. It is by nature a very personal thing and a well-loved collection is very much more interesting both to the owner and admirer than one formed haphazardly. If in any doubt about what to collect, there are many very good dealers who will be pleased to give both help and advice to an interested party—after all you are a potential customer!

FAKES AND FORGERIES

FAKES AND FORGERIES

The motivation behind most early fakes was usually political rather than financial, either because the smith or smiths involved had been expelled from the guild of their towns, or else because the plate in question was known to be sub-standard. As a result, fake marks are very scarce before the eighteenth century, but there is one type of fake mark which is to be found reasonably easily; this is a copy of the English marks, not only the marks of London, but the marks of all the provincial centres. These were fashioned by the expatriate English smith in the colonies in order to satisfy his patrons—most of whom were used to hall-marks—that his wares were of just as high standard as the hall-marked English wares; these marks usually date from the late eighteenth and early nineteenth century. It is illegal in this country to sell these pieces with what should be termed 'pseudo marks' as they are blatant copies of the legal assay marks.

The introduction of the duty in 1719 was, as has already been mentioned, instrumental in encouraging goldsmiths to transpose marks onto new pieces to avoid payment of the duty. However, although these pieces are technically 'fake' they are accepted as genuine to their period, and some pieces have been known to fetch more money because of the 'duty dodging' marks. It is not these *legitimate* fakes that the collector should be wary of because these only add interest to the collection, especially the colonial marks which are probably worth considerably more than their English equivalents.

It is remarkable that it was not until 1853 that an incredulous public was informed that there was nothing haphazard or modern about the date letters on silver plate, and that in fact these letters went back in regular cycles to the fifteenth century. This information, added to the already developing fashion for collecting 'old wares', led to a booming silver market in which for the first time the value of antique plate became inflated above its scrap price. The new collectors, however, were very ill-informed and a tremendous amount of faking was done. The most amusing fakes are the beautiful Elizabethan coffee pots which are to be found a good hundred years before coffee was first drunk in England; these have usually been fashioned by reversing damaged Elizabethan chalices and communion cups.

Another method of producing 'absurdities' was to transpose (in the manner of the duty dodgers) the marks of an earlier piece onto a supposedly 'antique' piece. This in particular led to the appearance of many very large casters of supposedly early eighteenth century origin, the only trouble being that they are quite considerably bigger than anything which was actually produced at that time. Pieces of this type are of little more than interest value and no reputable dealer will sell them.

Fakes and forgeries are very much the minority and with a little bit of practice in handling genuine plate a piece which is suspect will feel wrong. It is a very good rule not to buy unless absolutely sure that the

article is both something useful for a collection and completely in its original state. A
collector who follows this rule will find that
not only is the hobby rewarding in that each
individual item in the collection is a work of
art in itself, but the collection as a whole is
constantly appreciating in value.

REFERENCE

How to identify a piece and where to go to determine its origin, maker, uses and value is a question often asked. The answer is very difficult and frequently not found to be satisfactory. The main stumbling block is usually that the owner is equally interested in both identification and value, and both these queries can rarely be answered simultaneously.

Before trying to identify and value a piece it is necessary to overcome any mistrust of institutions—museums are there to help, not just to display material. There are one or more museums in every large town and their staff are completely trustworthy. They are always interested to be shown pieces in local possession and although they are not permitted to give their opinion as to value, will certainly be very helpful in determining as much as possible about the age, origin and original use of the piece in question. In the event of their being unable to give an immediate answer they will probably ask to be left with the piece in order to do further research, or alternatively will suggest where the owner will be able to find out more.

Antique shops do not like being asked to give free valuations for two reasons; the difference between valuation for insurance and valuation for sale is usually in the region of one hundred per cent, and it is part of a dealer's livelihood to charge for the service of using his professional knowledge to make a valuation. But a good dealer will be very willing to give his own personal opinion as to the identification of a piece so long as he isn't expected to offer a valuation at the same time.

There is a series of books published in the form of catalogues which help both in identification and price but these again are only expressing opinion and, although generally accurate, prices can tend to be on the high side, especially over the selling price. Reference to a sale room will ascertain an approximate estimate as to how much the piece will fetch at auction which, although very rough, does come from an agency which not only knows the current market trends but also helps to set them.

As regards reference books, there have of late been several publications, most of them very good, and it is up to the collector to choose those which bear most relevance to his subject. A small bibliography is contained at the back of this book.

CLEANING

CLEANING

There is more mystique and one-upmanship involved in the cleaning of silver than in practically any other part of the hobby. Really it is a great deal of fuss about nothing, for although some polishes are a little better than others, by definition the word polish means to rub. The only harm that any polish can do is to be slightly abrasive, and if common sense is used even the most abrasive polish will not render any harm to a piece after 50 years of continuous use.

Once a piece is polished it need not be polished again probably for as much as a year. All it needs is a wash in warm water once a week, and the drying-up cloth will do the rest without ever having to go near a tin of polish. If perfection is required, a cloth impregnated with silver polish can replace the drying-up cloth. The only achievement of a weekly polish is to wear out the decoration, and probably the marks on the item which is being subjected to this treatment, both of which detract from its value.

The best method for cleaning cast detail which so often becomes clogged with either polish or dirt is first to rinse the piece, however dirty, in a basin of really hot water; then brush out the dirt with a *soft* brush, an old tooth brush is ideal. Then if there is still tarnish left the best treatment is with liquid polish that is bought in bottles and which dissolves the tarnish; but when using this it is imperative that the instructions on the bottle are precisely followed, otherwise the silver can become discoloured.

Always be careful of the marks when using polish. They can usually be avoided, and it is worth remembering that a piece with worn marks is worth considerably less than a piece with clear marks which have been taken good care of. Put your thumb over the marks or stick a piece of tape over them, as this will afford the necessary protection while not hindering the polishing.

Silver-gilt should *never* be cleaned with anything other than a soft cloth and soap and water. If it still does not look clean, a handkerchief and a little literal 'spit and polish' can often help. Polish will remove the gilt in no time leaving silver shining through on all the points which are prone to wear. It is worth remembering that if a silver-gilt piece is genuine it will never be gilted anywhere which does not show or need protecting from erosion—like the inside of a salt-cellar—as gilding is very costly to put on, and the goldsmith was anxious to conserve his gold.

Another thing worth remembering is that tap water often contains a small proportion of chlorine, and if silver is left soaking in this too long or left wet after being taken out of the water it is likely to become discoloured.

When wrapping silver for storage bear in mind that if it is *well* wrapped it will not tarnish in store at all, and thus will not need to be polished when taken out. The best method is dry, acid-free paper, preferably black, wrapped round the silver, so as to completely isolate it from the atmosphere. This can then be wrapped in a sheet of newspaper, but it is essential that the newspaper does not touch the silver. The now fully wrapped piece of silver, insulated from bumps by the newspaper, should ideally be placed in a baize or polythene bag. Wrapped in this manner it should keep clean for years.

Do not wrap any gold items in paper however as this would affect the metal adversely. A simple layer of soft cloth should prove an effective means of keeping gold in good condition when stored. As with silver, gold plate and jewellery can be polished with a good quality polish though gentle washing in soap and water is an equally good way to keep the shine.

INSURANCE

INSURANCE

Having taken the trouble to collect silver, spending both time and money, it would be unfortunate and unnecessary to lose it all through fire or theft. Insuring silver, especially if it is valuable, is an expensive business. It is a good thing where a lot of silver is involved to have a detailed inventory made. Although seeming an extravagance this can be a very valuable investment; if properly kept up it will continue to be valid for a number of years as well as helping the police in the unhappy event of a burglary.

Having had your silver reliably valued you must then get in touch with insurers. It is best to go to an insurance broker, who will be able to find the best market and terms as he will be working in the interests of the insured. There is a list of brokers' addresses and telephone numbers in the 'Yellow Pages' Directory.

The rates charged vary minimally from

company to company. Up to £500 worth of silver may be insured under an ordinary Householders' Comprehensive Policy which most people hold to cover their domestic possessions. The premium for silver within the £500 limit is small. Over the value of £500 an 'All Risks' policy is required; the silver has to be listed with the value of individual items recorded to help both the police and the insurers in the event of theft or fire. It is well worth having any pieces worth £100 or more photographed, depositing one copy with the Insurance Company. An 'All Risks' policy is only valid while the silver is in a private dwelling. The premium is approximately double that under the Householders' Comprehensive Policy.

There is always the alternative of keeping the silver locked up at the bank where it can neither be used, seen, or admired and might just as well not exist, apart from the satisfaction of knowing that it is there. Silver kept in the bank should also be insured for the bank accepts no liability for damage by fire or loss by theft, so you must insure the silver yourself. Owing to the obvious security of a strong room the premium is proportionally lower, being about two thirds the price of the 'Comprehensive Policy'.

ENGLAND
(925·00 standard)

LONDON	PROVINCES
1180 Goldsmiths fined for not holding King's licence.	
1238 Six Wardens appointed to oversee craft.	
1327 Goldsmiths receive Royal Charter.	
1423 Leopard's Head mark introduced, makers' mark made legal necessity.	'Divers Touches' granted to Bristol, Coventry, Lincoln, Newcastle upon Tyne, Norwich, Salisbury and York.
1462 Goldsmiths become corporate body.	
1478 Variable date-letter introduced.	
1536 Dissolution of the Monasteries.	Dissolution of the Monasteries.
1544 Lion Passant introduced.	

LONDON	PROVINCES
1642 Civil War.	Civil War.
1660 Restoration.	Restoration.
1696 Britannia Standard introduced. Re-coinage commenced.	Britannia Standard introduced. Re-coinage commenced.
1700	Provision for Assay Offices at Bristol, Chester, Exeter, Norwich and York.
1702	Provision for Assay Office at Newcastle upon Tyne.
1717	Assay Office at York closed.
1720 Sterling Standard re-introduced. Duty of 6d an ounce started.	Sterling Standard brought back. Duty of 6d an ounce introduced.
1758 Duty taken off.	Duty taken off.
1773	Assay Offices opened at Birmingham and Sheffield.

LONDON	PROVINCES
1776	Assay Office at York re-opened.
1784 King's Head duty mark introduced with return of the 6d duty.	King's Head Duty mark introduced with return of 6d duty.
1856	Office at York closed.
1882	Office at Exeter closed.
1884	Office at Newcastle upon Tyne closed.
1890 Duty taken off; duty mark discontinued.	Duty taken off, duty mark discontinued.
1962	Office at Chester closed.

SCOTLAND
(916·6 standard)

EDINBURGH	PROVINCES
1457 Deacon appointed to place his mark alongside maker's mark on a tested piece.	
1555 Standard 'Restored' to 916·6.	Standard 'Restored' to 916·6.
1586 Goldsmiths granted their first Letters Patent.	
1681 Variable date letter introduced.	
1707 Act of Union.	Act of Union.
1720 Duty of 6d an ounce introduced.	
1758 Duty removed.	
1784 King's Head duty mark introduced with the re-imposition of 6d duty.	

EDINBURGH	PROVINCES
1819	Assay Office at Glasgow (925 standard).
1836 925 Standard made universal in United Kingdom.	
1890 Duty revoked and duty mark discontinued.	

CHRONOLOGICAL TABLE (3)

IRELAND
(925.00 standard)

DUBLIN	PROVINCES
1605 Maker's mark made legal obligation.	
1606 Mark of Lion, Harp and Castle introduced for assayed plate.	
1637 Goldsmiths granted charter of incorporation. Mark of Crowned Harp introduced for assayed plate.	
1638 Variable date-letters introduced.	
1730 Duty of 6d an ounce introduced, also figure of Hibernia duty mark.	
1752 Made illegal to sell plate without Hibernia mark.	
1784	Assay Office opened at New Geneva. Assay Office at New Geneva closed.

DUBLIN	PROVINCES
1801 Act of Union.	Act of Union.

1807 English duty introduced with King's Head duty mark.

1890 Duty revoked: duty mark discontinued.

1923 All plate after this date foreign in respect of Customs and Excise of the United Kingdom.

BIBLIOGRAPHY

General:

Report of the Departmental Committee on Hall-marking, H.M.S.O. 1959 (137 pp)

Silver, Gerald Taylor, Pelican, 1956 (302 pp)

English Silver, Judith Bannister, Ward Lock, 1965 (256 pp)

English Domestic Silver, Charles Oman, A & C Black, 1934 (240 pp)

Three Centuries of English Domestic Silver, Bernard and Therle Hughes, Lutterworth, 1952 (248 pp)

English Goldsmiths and their Marks, Sir Charles Jackson, Macmillan, 1921 (747 pp)

Special Periods:

Adam Silver, Robert Rowe, Faber, 1965 (190 pp)

Huguenot Silver in England 1688–1727, J. Hayward, Faber, 1959 (185 pp)

Also Victoria and Albert Museum series of Picture Books

Special Subjects:

Silver Boxes, Eric Delieb, Herbert Jenkins, 1968 (120 pp)

English Vinaigrettes, E Ellenbogen, Cambridge, 1956 (39 pp)

Bottle Tickets, Victoria and Albert Museum, 1958 (31 pp)

Price Guides:

Price Guide to Antique Silver, Ian Harris, Baron, 1968 (510 pp)

INDEX